TRACKINGS FROM THE SLED

Team Building Lessons From the Dogsled Team

Michael Bell

©Copywrite 2025 – NCompass LLC

Trackings From the Sled

Team Building Lessons From the Dogsled Team

Author: Michael Bell

ISBN 979-8-218-78288-7

Published by NCompass LLC

www.allncompass.com

Trackings From the Sled

Team Building Lessons From the Dogsled Team

Introduction

Chapter 1 - Dogsledding 101
(How a Dog Team Works)

Chapter 2 - Superstars
(A Great Pedigree Doesn't Insure a Great Team Player)

Chapter 3 - Lead, Point and Wheel Dogs Working Together
(Management Team Cohesion)

Chapter 4 - In for the Sprint or the Long Haul
(Racing Dogs Don't Make Good Freight Dogs)

Chapter 5 - Characteristics of the Lead Dog
(Knowing and Following the Voice Commands)

Chapter 6 - Tuffy
(Point Dogs Don't Always Make Lead Dogs)

Chapter 7 - Moving the Sled
(The Team Needs Steady Wheel Dogs)

Chapter 8 - Born to Run
(Finding What is Inherent)

Chapter 9 - Jealousy
(A Lead Dog in Heat is a Bad Idea)

Chapter 10 - Are They Really Pulling?
(Perfecting The Art of Making the Rope Taut)

Chapter 11 - It Takes the Whole Team
(Some May Need to Go Back to Camp)

Chapter 12 - Fixing the Sled with a Swiss Army Knife
(Use What You Have to Advance the Team)

Chapter 13 - The Unspoken Law of the Wilderness
(Leaving Kindling and Firewood for the Next Camper)

Chapter 14 – White Eggs and Snow are Identical in Color
(Traversing the Portages)

Chapter 15 - Following the Wolf
(A United Team Doesn't Guarantee the Right Direction)

Chapter 16 - Finding the Obliterated Trail
(The Team Finds Hidden Paths)

Chapter 17 - Falling Through the Ice
(Pushing Causes Disastrous Results)

Chapter 18 - Training the Puppies
(Apprenticeship Still is the Best Training)

Chapter 19 - Need to Mix it Up
(Freezing Winds can Bring the Team to a Halt)

Chapter 20 - Diamonds in the Snow
(Experiencing the Peace of a Harmonious Team)

INTRODUCTION

In the early seventies my wife Teresa and I joined an End-Time Community that felt strongly about the need to "get off the grid" and learn wilderness skills to prepare for anticipated world infrastructure collapses. We were, to all intents and purposes *"preppers"* before the term was coined 25 years later.

Living in log cabins on an electricity-free farm in northwestern Ontario and managing a 5-acre garden had multiple purposes – among them to learn homesteading skills and to become self-sufficient. We established three traplines 8 miles apart a hundred miles north via a narrow logging road deep in the woods. Tiny cabins on the traplines were hubs to facilitate harvesting martin and beaver furs as a source of income to fund and support the community.

One of my assigned duties prior to moving from our U.S. location to Canada was to develop a dogsled team to complement and provide logistics for the traplines during the trapping season.

The first dog team we purchased in southern New Hampshire came with a dogsled and all the harnesses and gear required to run the team. The sled was of the racing variety and in very bad repair. We needed a new heavier and longer freight sled to complement the team.

In the New Hampshire dogsled community, everyone knew the best place to get sleds repaired or to have a new sled fabricated - the "old cabinetmaker" in Peterborough. On my first visit to a cabinet shop, I learned his story. Mr. Davidson was a third-generation cabinetmaker with a traditional craftsman shop. Local mushers started bringing him their sleds to be repaired after the previous local sled builder passed away. After many years of building and installing cabinets, Mr. Davidson suffered a stroke which limited his ability to install cabinets. Because of the steady demand for dogsleds he found himself building them full-time.

On that visit I also apparently ingested some of his sawdust which resulted in my own love of wood and my lifetime career in the architectural woodworking industry. Mr. Davidson agreed to teach me the craft of dogsled building. Under his tutelage I fabricated our premium white ash freight sled that we took with us to Canada with the dog team.

This book is about many experiences and lessons I learned throughout all phases of training and operating the dog team. The dynamics and practicalities that can be learned in observing a dog team are astoundingly applicable regarding the interaction of people working together as a team.

The point about a dog team is, first and foremost it is a team. Second, it is a bunch of dogs with different personalities, hooked together by someone else, that are expected to pull in the same direction. It's not unlike the modern-day office (without the dog part in most instances). It is a group of varied individuals, each making a specialized contribution to corporately accomplishing a single goal. My point is not that people are like dogs, but to use the Leadership Trackings at the end of each chapter to extract practical management insights from the experiences shared.

(Any names used in this book are fictitious to guard the privacy of the individuals.)

Chapter 1

Dogsledding 101
(How a Dog Team Works)

Our first dog team was a collection of racing dogs from several kennels. They had not yet become a team, and I had not yet learned to be a trainer. After all, how hard can it be to hook up twelve dogs in tandem, get on the trail, shout "Mush!" and ride into the snow-covered sunset?
Well.......

The first thing to know about the dynamics of a dog team is that the team consists of dogs with different duties. The musher (the act of driving a team of dogs is known as mushing, and a person who participates is a musher) stays at the back of the sled and the dogs are stretched out in front of the sled connected to a single pull rope called a gang line. The dog harness has a connector in the back that hooks into an individual tug line coming out from that gang line. The line also has short connecting ropes that hook to the dogs' collars, referred to as neck lines. The tug line receives each dog's thrust and energy to pull the sled and the neck line maintains each dog in the tandem position.

Dogsled Team Positions

The functions of the different team members are basic:
- Lead Dogs - The front dog or in some instances pair of dogs are connected to the front of the gang line. They have no reins or connection to the musher. The lead dog is not counted on to pull as much as to control and to set the pace for the rest of the team. The lead dog is to keep the pull rope extended, set the pace for the team and set the direction of the team. The musher communicates with the lead dog with a series of voice commands:
    - *"Hike!"* which means get up and go (sorry if you thought mushers shouted out *"Mush!"* - it's actually *"Hike!"*).
    - *"Gee!"* which means turn right (an incremental right is *"Gee-a-Little!"*).

- *"Haw!"* which means turn left (along with *"Haw-a-Little!"*).
  - *"Whoa!"* probably the hardest command of all for the dogs to follow.
- Point Dogs / Swing Dogs - The next two dogs behind the lead are the point dogs. The duties of the point dogs are to assist the lead in turning the team and to help to set and maintain the pace.
- Team Dogs - Behind the point dogs are any number of pairs of team dogs. Team dogs are the worker dogs whose primary responsibility is to pull the sled.
- Wheel Dogs - The last two dogs closest to the sled are the wheel dogs. They need to be heavier because they provide the inertia to get the sled to start moving and provide the direct force to move the sled right or left.

Leadership Tracking: Understand Distinctive Roles

It is important for any group to recognize that each team member makes a different contribution to the efforts of the whole. It is imperative to have a leader who can direct the team in the right direction. But the leaders cannot be expected to pull all the weight themselves. They need help from the number twos who can assist in direction as well as helping to steer the team. And then there are others who are just as valuable but are more the worker bees – crunching out the work and steadily contributing to the momentum of the team. Pulling up the rear are those who can be counted on to do the heavy lifting. They have unique skills and abilities that can get any project started, keep it on track and help bring it home.

Even a fully functioning team needs a head coach who directs the whole lineup. This driver knows the overall course and executes the strategies to apprehend success. Where exactly are they going and how in the world are they going to get there? The director implements the game plan each step of the way. This head coach communicates to all the team members their distinctive roles and responsibilities as well as the overall group objectives.

Chapter 2

Superstars
(A Great Pedigree Doesn't Insure a Great Team Player)

The idea of twelve or more dogs, 30 to 40 pounds each, pulling a sled weighing up to three hundred pounds with the additional weight of the musher creates a situation where teamwork is a necessity - not an option. There must be a cohesive unit, maintaining momentum and working together to cover diverse terrain.

You might think that you want purebred dogs with outstanding credentials when selecting candidates for your team. With sled dogs the purebred registered breeds are Siberian Huskies, Malamutes or Samoyed Huskies. From a practical standpoint, most mushers will tell you that purebred dogs don't make the best team sled dogs.

There was a lot that I didn't know, including the fact that for the two types of teams —racing and freight - there are two very different temperament requirements. We were preparing a team for freight work on trails across frozen lakes. This would require dogs who are calm while still loving to run and pull. As we learned the ins and outs from other mushers, we learned that the larger breeds such as Alaskan Huskies or mixed husky breeds work best for this role.

Our first team that we obtained in New Hampshire were all purebred Siberian Huskies. They channeled their extreme excitement into running like banshees on the trails. It was quite challenging when I was first learning to hook the dogs up to their gang lines. The order of hooking up was to start at the back with the wheel dogs and move up the line until you reached the lead dogs. By the time I'd get the lead dogs hooked up, the working dogs in the middle would be so excited they would have their harnesses turned inside-out on the top of their backs. I never could figure out how they managed to get their feet out of the harness to do that!

Getting them to settle out of their uncontrollable excitement and focus on pulling together was extremely challenging. The more we learned from other mushers, we became aware that we needed to make some changes in our team "personnel". The high-charged intensity of the purebreds, with over-the-edge excitement and a lack of steadiness were going to be entirely counterproductive on a freight trail.

I think this dynamic exists because the purebred dogs come from a lineage where specific characteristics have been bred into the dogs. Those characteristics are all about enhancing the individual's specific conforming lines and traits. This is great for dogs who will be shown and rewarded with ribbons and numerous accolades. However, the traits for a sled team require the ability to fit in and contribute. These have not been important in the development of pure breeds.

An individual dog can be an award-winning superstar and be completely useless in a team environment. Keeping one's head down and just pulling are not considered valuable assets for pedigreed breeders.

Look at professional sports and see this same principle. Just being from an elite athletic school does not mean that one will excel at the professional level of the sport. And how often do athletes who go on to record setting careers have their roots with "second tier" schools? Most often the key to their success is teachability, hard work, and a heart to work with their teammates to achieve their team goals.

Leadership Tracking: Pick Performance over Pedigree

It is easy to recognize this application in business. While having an advanced degree from a prestigious business school can bring a lot of value, it does not necessarily make someone a good team player on the office team. Interaction and participation with others, handing off difficult tasks, or deferring to other methods and processes do not come from one's pedigree, but from a desire to work with others to achieve the corporate goals. A mixture of formal education and hands-on experience develops the qualifications for meaningful performance and results.

The truth is that most of the best team members are not superstars on their own. When the team members perform together as a cohesive unit, superstar results will be realized. For what superstar results are you preparing?

Chapter 3

Lead, Point and Wheel Dogs Working Together
(Management Team Cohesion)

When it comes to setting the course for the team, it would be a mistake to think that it is only the lead dog's role. Because the lead can establish direction she plays a very important role on the team. But the lead dog cannot move the entire team on her own. It takes the point dogs, the second in line, to move the team behind the leader. It is imperative that the point dogs learn to follow the musher's voice commands. This way the team is not only being led but also moved in the correct direction. The lead and point dogs can't adjust the direction of the sled without the assistance of the wheel dogs. It takes muscle to change the direction of a loaded sled. The wheel dogs need to respond to the commands and provide the torque required to steer the sled. The team simply won't work well without the lead dog, point dogs and wheel dogs all responding to the same commands.

As the musher, I would take the dogs one at a time from the hook-ups in the kennel, slip on the harness and hook the back ring of the harness to the individual tug line. Then I would hook the front of the harness to the neck lines. Once I got all the dogs safely attached to the lines and the gang line was fully equipped, I would go to the back of the sled and prepare for the business of the day's run. I'd make sure everything was fully loaded, strapped down and finally ready to start off on another adventure.

Once I pulled the hook out of the snow or ice, I was totally at the mercy of the dogs to take me where we needed to go. There was no steering wheel, rudder or sail. It was all dog power and all controlled by my voice. We would get to our destination only if I could communicate with these wonderful creatures where I wanted us to go. From our training sessions and previous trips, I knew that I had to have a leadership team. Each dog had a specific role, each playing an important and significant part in getting us on the right path and then keeping us on course. If my wheel dogs decided to go right and my point dogs wanted to go left, there was no way we were going to get anywhere. The good news was that the entire crew learned to mesh. As the leadership team awakened to their roles, the team dogs were contented to follow the route controlled by the leaders. This cooperation is inherent to the nature of these sled dogs and it was thrilling to experience when it all came together.

Leadership Tracking: Build a Cohesive Leadership Team

Any organization is like a dog sled team: the leadership needs to be shared by a group of individuals. There must be someone out front who regulates the course and adjusts any shifts needed to reach overall objectives. Behind this leader are several important people whose job is to steer the team. They need to synthesize the orders from up top and get the rest of the group in line behind the set directives. These "point dog" people need to be responsive and sensitive to Senior Management commands. They may not be out front, but they are essential in keeping the organization on track. Down the line are the "wheel dogs". These people do a lot of the heavy lifting, providing the heft needed to produce change. They steer the vehicle that propels the entire group. They are doers by nature and even though they follow the leaders, they set the pace for the rest of the team.

The members of the leadership group have a diversity of roles, duties and looks. They each must learn the commands and do their part in getting the entire team to its predetermined destination. They don't all look alike or assume the same role. It is essential that they all move in the same direction and respect each other's contribution to the leadership team.

Chapter 4

In for the Sprint or the Long Haul
(Racing Dogs Don't Make Good Freight Dogs)

The original dog team that we bought came from a dog sled racer who had picked his dogs to run in races popular throughout New Hampshire. These were ten-mile treks where the mushers wanted the dogs to sprint the entire distance. The idea was the faster the better, pulling an empty lightweight racing sled, keeping as nimble as possible. To meet this objective, several of the dogs were skinny and high-strung with a need for speed.

Our purpose for the dog team was very different - we needed to haul a longer and heavier freight sled with distance and endurance rather than being competitive in a race. I cannot fully express the frustration I had with these high-strung sprint dogs. Day after day when I wanted them to slow down to take precarious curves, they wanted to bolt out and see how fast they could take us through danger. When I wanted them to stop, they wanted to go like the devil. They were wound up and could only operate at one gear - wide open.

Don't get me wrong, these were great racing dogs and eventually made someone else a happy musher. I was just unsuccessful in making them overcome their breeding and previous training. I wanted "steady eddies", and these were "roadrunners". It took me a long time to realize that their behavior was not the result of my failure as a trainer but was a demonstration of what their nature permitted them to do.

Once I figured out the real problem was them, not me, I started replacing them with bigger, more even-tempered huskies. Putting the proper type of dogs in the right places transformed my team. In the end we would not have won any races, but we did get the gear and supplies delivered safely. A welcome bonus was that my frustration level dealing with the dogs was reduced to a pleasant and manageable level.

Leadership Tracking: Fit the Members to the Project

Picking the right team members is essential whether you are building a team from scratch, or you have inherited a team. Matching the best type of people for the specific kind of project will determine the outcome. Many short-term goals require fast-paced sprinters. Some people are exceptionally good at initiating tasks. They can set up the processes, organize the steps required and get the ball rolling. But these folks may lose interest and chafe at the bit to move on once things have been initialized. These ones may need to be replaced with those who have the temperament to deal with longer term more complicated tasks for this part of the project. They must be geared to go the long haul.

Understanding the project cycle and matching personnel that fit the needs will determine leadership success. Can you see where each of your personnel fit?

Chapter 5

Characteristics of the Lead Dog
(Knowing and Following the Voice Commands)

What qualifies a team dog to be a lead dog? Certainly, the dog needs to be willing to run up front and let the forward momentum continue throughout the entire run. But just running up front is not enough to be the leader. The most essential learned trait required to lead the team is understanding voice commands and executing them when they are called out.

Imagine driving a very long car with no steering wheel, no accelerator or brake pedals and only your voice to control your direction and ability to stop. That is what the musher experiences at the back of the sled. The dogs are spread out for quite a distance ahead and the only thing that drives the team is voice commands. When the leader responds and reacts all is well and results in an enjoyable and productive run.

The musher's shout-out "*Hike!*" must be followed with an enthusiastic lunge forward to get the team out of its starting stance and moving forward. Hesitation will result in any number of calamities (some of which are described in other chapters). An immediate response needs to come at each command.

A clearly uttered "*Gee!*" not resulting in a strong right turn can mean a life-or-death difference of following a solid trail or landing in a freezing cold river flowing under the visible ice surface.

The command "*Whoa!*" must result in the lead dog coming to a stop and halting the team.

The voice commands must be learned, and systematic training builds the rapport between the musher and the lead dog. A slight inflection like "*Gee-a-little!*" means just a gradual turn right. When traversing wide open frozen lakes these slight changes in commands make a big difference to ensure getting to the proper destination. Many sessions over weeks and months must be invested in the lead dog to teach her all the commands for her responses to become second nature. Repetitive exercises going over and over the directives eventually results in the lead dog guiding and keeping the team in control.

Leadership Tracking: Implement Clear Commands

Organizations must have their destination and course set from top management. Every leader within the group must become acutely aware of the signals from above to direct the team in the right direction with the pace needed to adapt to ever changing terrain. These signals can often be imbedded in policy directives or strategy discussions. Without the ability to "hear" at times subtle commands and to perform corrective maneuvers, the leader will cause costly delays and even thwart the team from succeeding in its mission. The rapport between senior management and team leader doesn't come overnight. Learning "voice commands" takes months and sometimes years. When the leaders consistently and faithfully implement the course directions amid treacherous trails the team will successfully get where they are intended to go.

Chapter 6

Tuffy
(Point Dogs Don't Always Make Lead Dogs)

Within a few months of getting the team and learning the first steps to being a musher we packed everything up, loaded the dogs into our newly built dog hauling box on the back of an old Willies Jeep and left for our new home in Northwestern Ontario.
On the way to Upsala, Ontario (a hundred miles west of Thunder Bay - north of Minnesota), we had engine trouble with the Jeep and were forced to spend the night at a motel outside of Buffalo, NY.

The dogs were safe in the dog box but there was no place to stake them out, so after taking them out singly for exercise, watering and feeding we bedded them down in the dog box. It was an extremely humid and hot summer night. Our seasoned lead dog Chinook shared a box with a great young puppy in training - Blaze.

We got up early the next morning and were devastated to find that Chinook and Blaze passed sometime in the night, apparently from heat stroke. We were crushed and upset with ourselves for having mechanical problems which resulted in our putting the dogs at risk.

We learned an invaluable lesson about caring for God's creatures and just how delicate life is. We never again had a problem with the care and protection of the dogs.

The sad result of Buffalo was that we lost not only friends we had made in Chinook and Blaze, but our lead dog and lead dog in training.

After setting up the kennel at our new home, my first task in working with the Alaskan Huskies was to train a new lead dog. Having a dog team without a lead dog is like having a car without a starter. It is ready to go, but just won't start. We still had Tatiana, a snow-white Siberian husky, but we needed more than one leader.

I learned the hard way that leadership is an inherent trait. The duties of the lead dog can be taught, but the ability to lead either is present or not. My case in point (pun not intended) is that while assessing the candidates for this all-important position, I observed that one of our point dogs - Tuffy, already knew voice commands and would assist in turning the team when I would call out "*Gee!*" and "*Haw!*" He would stop at the sound of "*Whoa!*" and had a good relationship with the other dogs on the team.

Everything I knew about a team said that raising up number two into the number one position was a sound and winning strategy. I was very excited about moving Tuffy into the lead dog position, giving him a great opportunity and a time saving process for me.

I went about the steps of entering the new era with my Tuffy-led team. I anchored the sled, hooked up the dogs starting at the back of the team. One-by-one I put on their harnesses and attached them to the pull rope. As I got closer to the front of the team, I got more excited about Tuffy. I finally got him hooked up and took my place at the back of the sled.

It was time for transition and to witness the leadership handoff that I was so expecting to see. I pulled up the grab hook and shouted out "*Hike!*" in my best authoritative voice and the team began to move. Did I tell you that huskies were born to run?

Tuffy froze and sat down, letting the rest of the team run him over. I called out to Tuffy, cajoled and encouraged him. He wouldn't budge. I am sure that it was a case of him not being able to lead rather than not being willing to lead. I tried several times, and my best efforts could not turn Tuffy into a lead dog. He was comfortable and a great contributor back in the pack but was overcome with fear when put in the front position.

Leadership Tracking: Recognize Born Leaders

Over the years, I have seen people promoted to leadership because they are great number twos and while the results may not be as drastic as the team overrunning them, the end results have been the same. My takeaway from Tuffy is that leadership is something that a person is born with or, as in Tuffy's case - not. You need to find the natural born leaders and develop them to apply that leadership to your organization.

Chapter 7

Moving the Sled
(The Team Needs Steady Wheel Dogs)

Becoming more acquainted with the team I was able to observe nuances regarding the various team positions. Each dog on the team participates in a different way. It didn't take long to recognize the invaluable contributions of our wheel dogs - Bartholomew and Shane. Even when the team was excited to start the run and all the dogs leapt at the command *"Hike!"*, it became obvious that without Shane and Bartholomew's efforts there would have been a slow start.

The wheel dogs are the two harnessed closest to the sled. They need several unique characteristics to provide inertia to get the sled moving forward and taking on the weight when turning the sled. They must be heavier than the normal team dogs and they need to have an even temperament to prevent sudden stops and starts. They also must know the voice commands *"Gee!"* and *"Haw!"* to start the turns as soon as possible to minimize binding.

When heavy snow falls during a run the double trail the sled creates fills in making the return trip more difficult to navigate. The situation becomes like a train without any tracks. Proven wheel dogs become invaluable in this type of situation. They keep the team moving steadily and establish new tracks. The harder the terrain the more value they contribute to the team. These are the "behind the scenes" warriors who keep the sled moving and turning in the right direction. They keep their heads down and just keep that steady dependable pull.

Leadership Tracking: Honor Your Support Members

There are people in every organization that are in every way the wheel dogs of that group. They carry gravitas without the need to be out front. In fact, they do better when staying in the back and steadily supporting the team. They "follow the commands" and help turn the momentum in the correct direction. Unfortunately, just like the wheel dogs they get taken for granted and even get more responsibility dumped on them because they are so faithful. But the team cannot reach its journey's end without these troopers. It never hurts to give the wheel dogs extra treats and even an additional scoop during feeding. This is a good lesson to apply in any group environment. Identify these folks and honor them even though they don't seek praise. Without good support members there will be a time when the team gets stuck. This can be prevented when the "wheel dogs" are engaged - resulting in the organization accomplishing its goals.

Chapter 8

Born to Run
(Finding What is Inherent)

One of the things I noticed working with Alaskan Huskies was their absolute love to run. They were ecstatic with the opportunity to pull the sled and head down the trail. When given the opportunity they displayed their love of participating with the team. From the moment they would see us heading to the gear shed, they would begin barking and jumping in their kennels. They leaped up and came alive once they were harnessed and heard the command "*Hike!*".

This was not forced upon them nor was it a response out of a required expectation. They just had within them a desire to run. The training came in teaching the commands and molding them into a cohesive unit.

It was apparent that they had within a natural propensity to be a part of the team. They genuinely liked to pull together and the further we ventured out the more they loved it. There would be no way you could put this group together and teach them to like what was expected of them - they just had it in them. This capacity was something bred into sled dogs. Years of their predecessors doing similar tasks in similar conditions resulted in a natural flow when the dogs ran together.

As a musher I just had to uncover what was inborn in these magnificent creatures. I quite simply just needed to hook them up and the "team" just happened. All the characteristics of a functioning crew unfolded as the dogs were allowed to just do what they loved to do. What was the "secret sauce" to putting diverse animals together and having a team develop as an outcome? The formula was letting what was inherent in them come out. It was creating an environment where the dogs could pull together and experience what their breeding preconditioned them to do. They just love to run.

Leadership Tracking: Let Them Run

When managing people in a team environment it is essential to take the time to learn what each person has inside of them. What do they love to do and what drives them when no one is looking? Everyone is different, but a universal longing within most people is to be a part of a functioning team. Often good management is getting out of the way and letting people be what they were born to be. Providing tools, guidance, direction and needed resources will create the context for a team to develop. Trying to make people do what they don't want to do is a formula for disaster. Achieving outstanding results in times of extreme pressure, whether it is compressed timeframes or unexpected complexity, is a direct result of letting the team kick into gear and rise to the challenge. There is something in the human psyche that meets challenges head on and performs at above expectation level. People just love to run. Let them!

Chapter 9

Jealousy
(A Lead Dog in Heat is a Bad Idea)

We had a white Siberian Husky with one blue eye and one brown eye. Tatiana was a very smart trained lead dog. She ran fast, knew her commands and had that slight swagger that drew respect from the rest of the mostly male team members.

I learned a lesson one day as I hooked up the dogs. I started in the rear, and one-by-one worked my way to the front of the team. As I took Tatiana from the kennel, I noticed the males on the team were showing an inordinate amount of interest in her. It was then that I realized she was in heat which is nature's way of propagating the canine species. I knew that she could still contribute her leadership role during this time and physically there wasn't any reason to leave her behind on this run.

However, I had not calculated the effect that her condition would have on the rest of the team. Several of our mild-mannered team dogs started exhibiting unusually aggressive behavior. They started lurching forward towards Tatiana even though the team was still anchored in a stop position. Next, they started to bare their fangs at each other with very aggressive growls while tangling up the lines with their erratic movements.

I voiced my displeasure by shouting out for them to stop and ordering them to behave. When I realized that the lines were tangled and I needed to intercede, I jumped into the middle of the action, grabbing one of them and then the other with the simple objective of getting them to calm down and to get the tug lines free from their twisted state. It was a rookie mistake for me to get into the middle of the situation. To this day I have a distinguished L-shaped scar on my left arm as a testimony to that day. My cool, calm and collected team dogs had turned into aggressive and wild beasts - clamping onto my arm as I policed the situation. The successful resolution to this dog-fight ruckus required putting Tatiana back in the kennel.

Leadership Tracking: Switch Out the Lead

Jealousy with a mix of alpha behavior can be devastating to a team. It will make otherwise great partners great disrupters. Backstabbing and "throwing others under the bus" are symptoms of jealousy and can stop a project's progress right in its tracks. Occasionally it is best to give the lead to someone other than your "favorite" - you will be able to avoid a resulting scar.

Chapter 10

Are They Really Pulling?
(Perfecting the Art of Making the Rope Taut)

This is one of the most profound things I learned from running dog teams and it took me several years to understand.

The dogs are hooked up in tandem and the two dog modules create the column. As each dog contributes, the combined thrust continually propels the sled forward across frozen lakes, wooded trails and portages between lakes. The sled cannot advance unless the team is working and expending the energy needed for movement.

The dogs are chosen for various positions relative to their physical build or mental characteristics. For instance, the larger dogs are put in the wheel position, closest to the sled, because they are key to moving the sled out of its stationery position. The point dogs are right behind the lead because they have acquired the skill of knowing the voice commands and helping the lead dogs to turn the team.

To measure the contribution of each dog I would observe the tug lines that connected the back of the dog's harness to the center gang line. If the lines remained tight, I concluded that the dog was pulling hard and contributing to the team effort. Whenever a slack developed it was time to see if the dog was hurt or distracted in some way. If distracted, usually a call out of the dog's name is enough to spur him back into his work mode and the line would tighten back up.

I did this regularly for months until one trip I needed to leave one of the team dogs behind due to a slight illness. I was surprised to find that with one less dog our progress did not suffer, nor did it appear that the other dogs were worse for wear at the end of the day. I began experimenting by shorting the team with various dogs on different days. Most of the dogs' absence resulted in slower times and more exertion on the others. But curiously two of the dogs seemed to have no effect on the progress of the team, whether with the team or left back at camp.

It was then that I realized those dogs had perfected the art of keeping the line taut: "pulling just enough to make the line tight but not enough to contribute to towing the weight". Truthfully, they were not contributing to the hauling shared by the rest of the team. As a result, I replaced those dogs with team dogs who actually helped to pull the sled. My lesson learned;

I consequently watched for this slacker characteristic in any of the dogs.

Leadership Tracking: Flush Out the Slackers

Over the years I noticed in business that there are occasionally team members who contribute the bare minimum to the overall workload. They have "perfected the art of keeping the line taut" by always appearing to be busy in front of the boss. When under observation, they put up the signs of "pulling". Unfortunately, an individual covertly making themselves indispensable to the organization without really contributing to the team effort is not a rare phenomenon in many workplaces. What do you think, have you seen this type of behavior?

Chapter 11

It Takes the Whole Team
(Some May Need to Go Back to Camp)

Typical January temperatures at our latitude ranged from zero to 30 below (F). It was very cold, even colder than normal, when I hooked up the dogs for the trek across the lakes to transport supplies to the next cabin. There were extreme winds and the snow blowing up from the lake made almost white-out conditions. The usual exuberance from the dog team was missing and to the point that several of the dogs resisted being harnessed and set out on the gang line.

This was highly unusual since the number one joy of sled dogs is to get out and run. But this day was different. No matter how hard I tried, four of the sixteen dogs refused to stand in line with the team. I did the only thing I could do, I let those dogs loose and they bee-lined back to our camp. I realized that the important thing about the team is that every member needs to pull his share. It is far better to run with twelve dogs participating than to have the whole team dragged down by four unwilling souls.

This same day, once we got underway and headed out across the lake, the vapor from my breath traveled up my face and caused my eyelids to freeze shut. I had never heard of this phenomenon let alone experienced it. No wonder some of the dogs balked about coming out with us that day! I slipped off one of my goose-down gloves and pinched my eyelids with my much warmer fingers. The heat of my hand caused the ice to melt, and I could finally open my eyes to see.

The dogs and I were extremely happy several hours later when we arrived at our associated cabin. I noticed the harsher than normal conditions caused the participating team members to pull a little harder and run a little faster to get to our destination that frigid afternoon.

Leadership Tracking: Only Work with Willing Participants

The dynamics of synergy is the interaction or cooperation of two or more agents to produce a combined effect greater than the sum of their separate effects. The lesson I learned from the sled that day is that when all the agents are willing to work together, even with a reduction, the results can eclipse forcing unwilling participants to be dragged along.

There are times when it is better to let your balking team members go. Not every team member who starts out with you will want to face your hardships and downturns. Sometimes organizations go through tough spots and not everyone wants to work as hard as it takes to make it through. Just as it takes prolonged heat to temper steel, the synergy of a team that is forged in hardship will come out stronger in the end. Embrace those willing to tough it out and be willing to restructure your team when the trying times warrant the winnowing of unwilling participants.

Chapter 12

Fixing the Sled with a Swiss Army Knife
(Use What You Have to Advance the Team)

I was privileged to work with a third-generation cabinet builder to construct our white ash freight sled prior to moving to our Canadian homestead. I became familiar with the processes involved in cutting, steaming and bending wood components, lashing together all the parts to make a sled flexible enough to withstand the rough Canadian wilderness.

When I ventured out past the edge of civilization, I did not prepare for the tools that I would need if the sled broke. My Swiss Army knife was the only tool I packed for our six-week venture. It was a full featured model and included the standard bottle opener along with a saw blade and an awl that could poke holes in leather.

When running the team through some irregular underbrush one of the sled's runners snapped off about fourteen inches from the end. I was able to make it back to camp without any major problems but needed to address the sled repair before going out again the next day.

The only solution I could find to make the sled functional again was to cut off the other runner to make both sides even. I needed new holes to allow proper lashing of the upright stantions to the back of the sled with the shortened runners.

My only tool was my Swiss Army knife. I took the sled into the very small cabin and began the arduous task of rebuilding the rear end of the sled without the luxury (and arguably, necessity) of a fully outfitted cabinet shop. Each step of the re-fabrication process was slow and tedious. Using the little saw to trim the hard white ash, drilling holes with a leather awl and re-lashing the components took hours. Accomplishing the same tasks in a woodshop would have taken only a few minutes of effort.

Finally, with the repair exhausting most of the day, the sled was now in a usable state again, even if somewhat shorter. What looked like a season ending mishap to the freight sled wound up being only a bothersome setback, thanks to that Swiss Army knife!! I'm sure that my true story would make a great testimonial advertisement for the Swiss Army folks. I used that knife for a bit more than it was engineered to do, but with it I managed to get us back on the trail.

Leadership Tracking: Use the Resources You Have

There are times when the "best laid plans of mice and men" just get derailed. In moments like these, we don't necessarily have the "proper" resources or tools to fix the problems. A true leader will inventory the resources in hand and begin the exercise of "thinking outside the box" to develop a repair plan. Having a "can-do" attitude will often result in solving problems in unorthodox ways. Too often people give up when their solution is right in front of them, disguised as a Swiss Army knife. When have you used your Swiss Army knife?

Chapter 13

The Unspoken Law of the Wilderness
(Leaving Kindling and Firewood for the Next Camper)

In the previous chapter I told the story of re-building the freight sled with my Swiss Army knife. Spending the day on repairs meant a late start in leaving the cabin to head eight miles across several lakes to another cabin. Darkness comes early in the afternoon in the Canadian winters. We were on a tight time frame, and I needed to set out despite the oncoming darkness. Midway between the cabins was an outfitter's lakeside fishing camp. The cabin was constructed of a lightweight plywood shell with the upper walls and roof made of canvas. It was a perfect spot for float plane fly-in summer excursions.

Because of the late start and frigid cold, I decided to spend the night at this midway point. In the dark I drew the dog team up to the fishing camp and stretched out the gang chain used to park the dogs when out on the trail. Time passed as I detached the dogs' harnesses and hooked them up prior to their feeding and watering. Upon completion, my plan was to light the stove, grab a bite of dried food and down a bit of coffee before unfurling my goose-down sleeping bag for the night.

Upon entering the fishing shack, I quickly saw that the unspoken law of survival in the wilderness had been neglected by the previous visitor: *"ALWAYS leave kindling and wood in the stove ready to light, for the next person"*. There was no kindling left for me to start a fire. And there were only two large diameter logs left in the log bin.

I went outside past the sleeping curled up dogs to retrieve kindling from the nearby pine trees. What I hadn't considered was the many forays into the surrounding woods by summer campers harvesting kindling and wood for their campfires. As far as I traversed the perimeter of the fishing camp and as deep as I went into the woods, there were no small branches left on the pine trees. The long and short of it is there wasn't any kindling to be found that night.

A slight panic set in as the cold intensified and I wondered how I was going to endure the double-digit sub-zero night, protected only by the canvas-topped dwelling. I am not proud of the next part of my story, but I proceeded out of survival necessity.
When I re-entered the cabin after my unsuccessful search for kindling, I noticed that there was a sink on the porch installed to be used for cleaning fish. Someone had propped up the sink with a short softwood 2x4. Upon spotting that wood, I reluctantly

removed it from under the sink. Next, I split it into kindling with my hatchet. It successfully ignited and generated enough heat to light one of the logs. I unpacked my dinner, stretched out the sleeping bag and downed a cup of now cold coffee. The first log helped to warm things up but only for an hour or so. I looked at the stove, decided to put on the last log and then crawl into my sleeping bag. I remember the thoughts I had when putting on the last log - "It's going to be really cold in the morning".

I finally fell asleep. When I awoke, I got dressed and immediately went to pour a cup of coffee. Then I realized the liquid in the Thermos was frozen solid, I gave up on breakfast and headed back out with the dogs to deliver the needed supplies. We eventually made it back to our camp without loss, but it is an experience I wouldn't want to repeat.

Leadership Tracking: Prepare for the One Who Follows

Think about the person who receives your work. Sometimes ten minutes of your time will save hours for the person coming behind you. An effective leader understands this principle and never leaves a task complete without "setting it up" for the persons following. The unspoken law of survival in the wilderness, leaving kindling and firewood for the next camper, applies in every organizational environment. There is always someone receiving your work. Labeling and leaving a trail will often save that person following a lot of grief and heartache. It can mean the difference of success or failure for the entire group. Leave some kindling and firewood. It may just save a life when a 2x4 may not be available.

Chapter 14

White Eggs and Snow are Identical in Color
(Traversing the Portages)

Our trapline cabins were about eight miles apart, separated by lakes. Rather than travel along random shorelines of the frozen lakes, we established portages (stretches of land between the lakes) that would make our routes more direct. Some of our fellow trappers were working out of another cabin. One of my duties with the dogs and sled this season was to transport supplies and food to those who had already spent six weeks out ahead of us. While spending weeks isolated in the cold wilderness, even small amounts of special food can be a delightful treat.

Before heading out, I placed a cardboard box containing twelve dozen eggs on the sled. I had let the eggs freeze by leaving them outside in the sub-zero air. The only downside with thawing out frozen eggs is they can no longer be served sunny-side up or over-easy. The yolks would harden like hard boiled eggs. They still were a treat and offered a great alternative to oatmeal for breakfast.

We started the day's trek heading across a frozen lake. The dogs settled into their steady lope, and we were clocking pretty good time. We approached the first portage that had been cleared earlier in the summer on an extended canoe trip. While I had worked hard to clear the paths on the portage with a chain saw, I was unable to eliminate the abrupt ups and downs in the trails.

Once the dogs headed into the portage trail, they sprung alive and started darting down the path. Slowing the dogs down through any wooded trail was always a challenge. This specific jog had a steep incline heading down. The dogs considered this an opportunity to race and picked up speed as we crossed a hump and headed down.

Using the brake, shouting commands to slow down and holding on for dear life, I watched, as if in slow motion, as the sled headed up in the air and then flipped on its side. Everything in the sled spilled out as we careened down the steep slope. I watched in horror as traps, gear and cartons of food flew into the woods.

After I got the dogs stopped and the sled upright, I noticed the box of eggs. The top had torn open and about half of the eggs were gone, sprinkled throughout the snow. Picking up the eggs one-by-one I realized it was going to be a long tedious exercise. After recovering a dozen or so eggs, a fact I never realized before dawned on me – white eggs and snow are identical in color. It's a fact that has not helped my life since, but at that time it contributed to the difficulty of finding all the eggs. After I finished loading the sled back up and got the team eased through the balance of the portages and lakes, I happily learned that my friends were delighted to receive even ten dozen eggs!

Leadership Tracking: Slow Down in the Transitions

There are times of transition with all organizations. Change of supervisors, new projects, ownership change or change of location are just a few factors. Any transition can cause uncertainty, unnecessary or unplanned activities that can bring on undue risk. The best course of action during these transition periods is to slow things down. It is better not to make dramatic moves that could upset the balance in the group. The rush to complete the present course prior to the change taking place could mean you will be forced to retrieve eggs from the snow. Any number of your goals may blend into the background and get lost because of haste. On top of that, your customers may find it unacceptable to be short changed.

Chapter 15

Following the Wolf

(A United Team Doesn't Guarantee the Right Direction)

One sunny day I was heading out across a frozen lake with the team. The night's snow blanketed the terrain, and I noticed we were leaving behind a distinguished trail. The strong blowing wind began obliterating the tracks for our return trip. One of the amazing traits of the dogs, however, was that even if the trail gets blown over, they manage to pick up the previous trail and follow it.

We were loping along in the crisp, sunny afternoon. I looked out ahead and noticed a timber wolf trekking across the same lake we were crossing. The wind was blowing in the opposite direction which meant that the dogs did not pick up the scent until we were right up on the wolf.

When the wolf smelled the dogs, he headed straight for the woods. Needless to say, the dogs headed for the wolf, following at breakneck speed. There was no slacker in the bunch. They all decided that the wolf had a better idea of where we needed to go than I did as the musher.

I disagreed with their hijacked course and needed to bring the team to a halt before we got into the thick forest where there were not any trails. This was an instance when the power of a strong "Whoa!" was effective. That command with a strong stomping on the brake halted our forward momentum. Much to the dogs' displeasure, I rerouted them across the lake, resuming our original course. They continued to strain to look in the clearing where the wolf disappeared into the woods, but we avoided a potentially catastrophic situation and were now heading in the correct direction.

Leadership Tracking: Don't Follow Groupthink

It is up to the leadership team to set the course of any organization. Much has been said and taught about "consensus" leadership but just like in the wolf example, there are times when the entire team can head off in the same direction and it can be contrary to the prescribed course. It is important that leadership continually nudges the group into the correct route. And there are even times when a strong "Whoa!" may be needed. Those in leadership must be willing to take strong action to prevent the entire team from getting lost in the woods. Don't you find that sometimes it's best to just let the wolf get away?

Chapter 16

Finding the Obliterated Trail
(The Team Finds Hidden Paths)

Taking the dog team across the lakes meant following established routes. We travelled across snow that had been packed during previous trips. This made traveling easier than going through new drifts and forming fresh trails.

We had an issue with persistent blizzards. As it stormed, our trails would be obliterated with the fresh snowfall. Looking out across the lake it was impossible to see the best route for the team to travel. The dogs leading the team instinctively knew where the padded trail fell beneath the crystal cover. They would follow the previous trail and get us to our destination with relative ease.

I never understood how they did it, but every time they followed exactly. I'm not sure how it would have worked if the dogs didn't have the ability to know where the packed route was hidden. We would have been forced to make new trails each time we ventured out. The effort it would have taken to continually plow through over a foot of powdery snow would have put a lot of additional stress on the team. Our distance per hour would have been cut in half and our maximum daily traverse would have been considerably shorter.

Once I understood that these dogs could follow hidden established trails, I began to trust them more and more. We would travel the same routes every few days as we delivered supplies and picked up the furs that had been harvested. It was reassuring to know that even with the fresh fallen snow and wind-generated drifts we could still take the most direct paths. We did not have any GPS devices back then but somehow the dogs had their own internal GPS that kept us in line and assisted us in getting where we needed to go.

Leadership Tracking: Establish Processes

Establishing processes in an organization removes the guessing game of how to accomplish desired results. Once your team has been oriented to follow established processes they can perform even when a changing landscape transpires. Change is inevitable in today's world - personnel, customers, projects, regulations and technology, to name a few. These can act as steadily falling snow, obscuring the routes to previous successes. By setting in place procedures that transcend any changes in people or resources you will experience your team finding the course that delivers you exactly where you want to go.

Chapter 17

Falling Through the Ice
(Pushing Causes Disastrous Results)

One full moon night we were approaching our deadline to get our furs picked up and prepare for our extraction from the wilderness. With plenty of moonlight I had confidence that I could see clearly enough to keep us on track to the other cabin. We had been traveling steadily throughout the days but when the opportunity presented itself to traverse at night, I took advantage of it. The dogs always welcomed a good run and had no problem heading out into the well-lit night. It was surreal to follow our trail with the snow-covered lake reflecting the glow of the moon. Life was good as we progressed towards our end point.

What was not perfectly illuminated was where a river flowed out into the lake. Frozen snow-covered watercourses blended, and it wasn't until the much lighter dogs crossed the frozen river that I realized the sled was over the much thinner ice. The lake ice was solid for several feet, but the river ice was undermined by the flowing water beneath. My weight caused the river ice to crack and break open. I found myself slipping down into the cold water beneath and losing control of the dog team. My mind kicked into survival mode, as I knew it was a matter of life or death to get back above the ice.

What started out as a magical night journey changed in an instant to an extreme moment of truth. Everything slowed down, but I did not panic. I reached up and found that the ice sheet around the hole I was in was thick enough to allow me to grab hold and shimmy up out of the frigid water. Apparently, it was not my time to perish as I found myself out of the water and back on top of the ice. Inexplicitly the dogs had stopped after I fell off the sled and were available to transport me back to camp. I was very blessed that hypothermia did not set in and that I safely made it to back to the warmth of the cabin.

Leadership Tracking: Don't Over Push Your Team

There are times when looming deadlines cause us to push our teams beyond normal stress levels. Extended overtime or weekend work may seem like the only solution to getting things done in time. But pushing people, systems or equipment may result in the opposite of what is wanted. Breakdowns, sickness or compounded stress failures will delay reaching the goal every time. A good leader will recognize when their people have reached max output and will recalibrate rather than experiencing the unintended consequences of overtasking. Falling through the ice will bring the project to a halt every time and can sometimes be unrecoverable. Have you ever fallen through the ice and disrupted your team goals?

Chapter 18

Training the Puppies
(Apprenticeship Is Still the Best Training)

We bred several of the dogs and were rewarded with a healthy litter of little dog sled puppies. We learned that the nature of the sled dog is bred in - they come into this world with it as a part of their DNA. They want to run and want to pull. We were very careful not to make them a part of the team too early. We found that allowing the young dogs to run alongside the sled was an excellent way to train them. They would be right next to the big dogs. And while they were not expected to pull, they did learn to keep up with the rest of the team. As much as they loved to run, keeping up was seldom a problem.

We would limit each trip to the number of puppies we would take to be able to concentrate on helping just those dogs to learn the ropes (literally). It was fun for the puppies, fun for the team dogs and fun for us. To learn to run with the team was an off shoot of their stint out on the trail. Learning by doing was the best prescription for incorporating the young ones in with the seasoned veterans.

Over a three-year period, we cared for a total of 52 different dogs, including a variety of pups that we raised and trained. Working with the puppies was one of the most enjoyable parts of the mushing experience.

Leadership Tracking: Rediscover Apprenticeship

The true meaning of apprenticeship has been lost in our culture, but it hasn't always been this way. The system of apprenticeship was first developed in the later Middle Ages and came to be supervised by craft guilds and town governments. The Master Craftsman was never fully recognized as a Master until he had trained and apprenticed others. He was entitled to employ young people as an inexpensive form of labor in exchange for providing food, lodging and formal training in the craft. Formal programs existed, but most often the learning took place as the young person worked side-by-side with the seasoned veteran. It was not uncommon to take four to six years for the newcomer to grasp the essentials of the trade from the teacher.

Side-by-side learning, like the pups observing and mimicking the masters, works today just like it did in years past and just like it did on the trap line. Are you able to train the young pups in your system?

Chapter 19

Need to Mix it Up
(Freezing Winds can Bring the Team to a Halt)

Our trapping would start once the lakes froze over, making the navigation throughout the wilderness achievable. Once the portages (stretches of land between lakes) were connected by the frozen snow-covered lakes we could travel without obstructions across the terrain.

We would stay out in the trapping cabins for six week stretches, giving us an optimum trapping season. Our traplines were about one hundred miles north of the Trans-Canadian highway via a logging road up through the wilderness. At a designated milepost there was a logging camp where the semi-trucks originated their treks coming down the primitive road. Think "Ice Road Truckers" with massive loads of tamarack and pine logs. Our point of departure to the trap line was several miles up from the logging camp.

Upon arrival at our access, we would unload our trucks and then take them empty to park at the camp until trapping season was over. There was a place for us to plug in our block heaters when it was time to leave. The average temperature during our trapping season was 30 below zero (F). We had never heard of "wind chill factor", so we went with the actual readings. It was interesting to note that the thermometer that was proudly displayed on the side of our little base cabin had dropped so low it broke the bulb and gave us little hint of any presiding temperature.

As a safeguard we had a pre-set date when our associates were scheduled to meet us at the start of our trail. They would help us get back down to the logging camp and jumpstart our trucks. This generated a hard deadline for us to get all gear and furs to the rendezvous point.

With a sled full of gear to be taken out, I headed out to traverse the eight miles from our cabin to the road. The start of the trail was across a wide-open frozen lake and things started out smoothly. I noticed that it felt especially cold, but I had no choice but to proceed with only a few short days left in our season. The dog team traveled several miles until we crossed a short piece of land jutting out to the next part of the lake. As soon as we came out of the trees, I felt a strong cold wind pick up. It hit head on as we left the protection of the forest. I wasn't the only one who felt the frigid blast. I had never experienced this before and never since, but when the whole team got out on the snow-covered ice, they stopped dead in their tracks and every single dog laid down. They curled up with their noses tucked into their hind legs.

I shouted out the magic start trigger, "*Hike!*". Nothing. "*Hike!*". Nothing. "*Come on you guys, get up!*" Nothing.

My voice raised with each utterance, and I was met with the same response. So, I ran up to the front of the team and tried to pull the lead dogs to get them started. Panic started as I realized I could end up stranded in the treacherous cold without the dogs' cooperation and I gave them a good piece of my mind. And at the time my mind wasn't fixed on sweet melodies. I tried one by one to get at least one of the dogs to start back up and face the extreme wind. Still nothing.

This was a moment in my own life that I lost it. I am not proud of it, but I shouted some not so nice things to the team. Standing at the back of the sled and having absolutely no control in the situation I started to look up and question the Man Above. And then I spurted out some not so nice things to Him. "What am I doing in the middle of this dire situation and how come I find myself at the end of the rope?"

When I finished with my own Job-like moment I stopped and just waited. Several minutes went by until my panic subsided. At that point, in a perfect calm, it came to me to move the dogs around on the team. I put team dogs in the lead position and switched out much of the team.

Once I got the team moved around, I stood on the back of the sled, unhooked the brake and shouted out steadily, "*Hike!*" Every dog on the team stood up and started pulling. After I gave a quick but sincere prayer of gratitude, we headed out to our drop off point. I had no more problems in the subsequent days, and we met our associates several days later with all our gear and furs at the pick-up spot. The first thing they told us was that they were plenty worried about us since the temperature had dropped to forty-five below zero (F) with gale force winds.

Leadership Tracking: Reassign for Restarts

There are times when the winds of adversity blow across our projects and bring the team to a halt. Whether you experience unrealistic deadlines or money losing patches, there are situations that can completely lock up your team. Looking for the catalyst to solve extreme problems may appear bleak. If you sincerely ask for divine help and are open for unique solutions (that may include reassigning responsibilities), they just could put the whole project back on track. Mixing it up may have amazing results when the normal processes are at a standstill.

Chapter 20

Diamonds in the Snow
(Experiencing the Peace of a Harmonious Team)

Riding on the back of a sled crossing a frozen lake covered with snow and hearing only the pattering feet of thirteen dogs, with the sun piercing the cold air and shining down on the frozen ice particles, a surreal feeling overtakes you. The snow glistens as if covered by thousands of diamonds. A peace prevails over the silence, the loping of the dogs causes the sled to feel like it is floating across the frozen expanse. It is a totally unique feeling as you move forward, creating your own trail.

An almost hypnotic atmosphere develops as the minutes pass to hours. The dogs move in unison, running forward as one entity and a rhythm develops. It is cold but majestic and you think about how pristine it is - no trash, no pollution of noise or other man-made waste. There is just something about the team coalescing, all members pulling their load - a true synergy propelling you forward to your eventual destination. The dogs seem to catch the spirit in the air and continue to exert themselves for the sake of the team. To be part of this is a beautiful thing.

The awe it inspires rivals the feelings of an elaborate gothic cathedral. It is peace with just a little sting on your nose.

Leadership Tracking: Attain Harmony

When your organization begins to fire on all cylinders and you are moving forward without the distractions and hindrances that are caused by having gaps in human resources, you begin to see longtime corporate goals being met. Profit and positive cash flow result. Lower turnover and higher productivity come into play. You see your group becoming industry leaders, creating new paths in uncharted territories. When the team gels, something magical happens. Nothing else is like the experience of that harmony. Excuses are no longer needed. Races are won and result in championships. When all participants do their part and work together with the rest of the team, accomplishments are guaranteed. The true reward isn't just reaching the finish line, but the quiet, unspoken beauty of a team in perfect harmony, like diamonds shining in the snow. Can you see how this might happen for you?

Mike Mushing in Canada

Mike with First Dog Sled

Mike's Dog Sleds For Sale

Author

Michel Bell has been involved in the Architectural Woodwork industry for over 50 years. He is an accomplished Cabinetmaker and has owned two successful Commercial Woodworking Businesses and has worked as an Estimator, Project Manager and General Manager. He is currently working in his company NCompass, LLC - a Woodworking Management Training Company. He is highly recognized and considered an expert in the woodworking field, incorporating craftsmanship and business acumen.

www.allncompass.com

www.ingramcontent.com/pod-product-compliance
Lightning Source LLC
Chambersburg PA
CBHW042337040426
42446CB00021B/3479